THIS WALKER BOOK BELONGS TO:

_____

_____

_____

_____

For Emily and Giles Woolley

First published 1985 by
Walker Books Ltd
Walker House
87 Vauxhall Walk
London SE11 5HJ

This edition published 1988

Reprinted 1988

Printed in Hong Kong by
Sheck Wah Tong Printing Press Ltd

British Library Cataloguing in Publication Data
Hughes, Shirley
Noisy.—(Nursery collection).
1. Noise—Juvenile literature
I. Title   II. Series
620.2'3   TD892
ISBN 0-7445-0923-8

Noisy

Shirley Hughes

WALKER BOOKS
LONDON

Noisy noises!
Pan lids clashing,

Dog barking,
Plate smashing,

Telephone ringing,
Baby bawling,

Midnight cats
Cat-a-wauling,

Door slamming,

Aeroplane zooming,

Vacuum cleaner
Vroom–vroom–vrooming,

And if I dance and sing a tune,
Baby joins in with a saucepan and spoon.

Gentle noises...
Dry leaves swishing,

Falling rain,
Splashing, splishing,

Rustling trees,
Hardly stirring,

Lazy cat
Softly purring.

Story's over,
Bedtime's come,

Crooning baby
Sucks his thumb.

All quiet, not a peep,

Everyone is fast asleep.

MORE WALKER PAPERBACKS

BABIES' FIRST BOOKS

Jan Ormerod
Baby Books

READING   SLEEPING

DAD'S BACK   MESSY BABY

PICTURE BOOKS
For The Very Young

Helen Oxenbury
Pippo

No. 1 TOM & PIPPO READ A STORY

No. 2 TOM & PIPPO MAKE A MESS

No. 3 TOM & PIPPO GO FOR A WALK

No. 4 TOM & PIPPO AND THE
WASHING MACHINE

No. 5 TOM & PIPPO GO SHOPPING

No. 6 TOM & PIPPO'S DAY

No. 7 TOM & PIPPO IN THE GARDEN

No. 8 TOM & PIPPO SEE THE MOON

LEARNING FOR FUN
The Pre-School Years

Shirley Hughes
Nursery Collection

NOISY

COLOURS

BATHWATER'S HOT

ALL SHAPES AND SIZES

TWO SHOES, NEW SHOES

WHEN WE WENT TO THE PARK

John Burningham
Concept Books

COLOURS   ALPHABET

OPPOSITES   NUMBERS

Philippe Dupasquier
Busy Places

THE GARAGE   THE AIRPORT

THE BUILDING SITE

THE STATION   THE HARBOUR

THE FACTORY

Tony Wells   Puzzle Books

PUZZLE DOUBLES

ALLSORTS